Bursting out in Praise

SPIRITUALITY & MENTAL HEALTH

GAVIN THOMAS MURPHY

First published in 2019 by Messenger Publications

ISBN: 978 1 78812 085 2

Scripture quotations are from New Revised Standard Version Bible,
copyright © 1989 National Council of the Churches of Christ in the
United States of America. Used by permission.
All rights reserved worldwide.

Designed by Messenger Publications Design Department
Typeset in Stevens Tilting Pro, LTC Caslon, Beyond The Mountain
Printed by Johnswood Press Ltd

Messenger Publications,
37 Lower Leeson Street, Dublin 2
www.messenger.ie

CONTENTS

≡ ● ≡

≡ ● ≡

INTRODUCTION

Mental-health professionals have long taught us that wellbeing exists on a continuum, spectrum or scale of functioning. At the lowest end of the continuum, we find life a real struggle and we find it hard to cope. When we are feeling OK, toward the middle of the spectrum, we experience the ups and downs of life, but we have the tools to cope with the challenges. When we are feeling well, toward the higher end of the spectrum, we are enjoying and relishing life to the full.

From a *contemplative* perspective, we experience turmoil when we are turned away from God and, sometimes, we must fight tooth and nail to return to the light. Conversely, we feel serene when we are in tune with an inner stillness, and are familiar with the inner workings of God.

My own story may serve a purpose here. While I was volunteering in Guyana, South America in 2007

I experienced a 'triple whammy': I came down with a fever, suffered an accident and experienced a personal loss. At the time, I did not have the skills to cope; I got lost in distractions that kept me feeling low. I returned to Ireland and struggled for months on end. I found my physical and mental symptoms too much to handle, and later I experienced depression. I now refer to this period as a 'dark night of the soul'; I recall kneeling among the sand dunes near where I live and crying out: 'My God, my God; why have you forsaken me?' I hoped that someone was listening to me.

I found the inner strength to endure and came to work in Dublin again. However, I was quite sensitive about recalling my Guyanese experience to people because I was still caught up in the memory of the pain. Sometimes my friends seemed entertained by my 'triple whammy', but I found it difficult to join in on the laughter. As I began to grow in my spiritual life, I was able to get some distance from my pain and to tune into another perspective.

This booklet also attempts to tune into another perspective: it examines a range of experiences associated with mental health and wellbeing with the aim of pointing to something 'more'. I claim that our inner dynamism – with the application of tools and resources – even calls us to 'burst out in praise' in the midst of our pain or suffering.

I have decided to use examples of my own mental health experience in the hope that they help others on their journey. I have bipolar disorder, a condition known for its changes and challenges in mood, such as depression, low mood, dysphoria (intense unease and agitation), hypomania (elation and overactivity) and mania. I hope that the reader may relate to my experience in the knowledge that we are all somewhere on the mental health continuum. Research shows, for example, that anxiety and depressive symptoms are incredibly common in the general public, and that many people hear voices occasionally or have fears or beliefs that they do not share with those around them. My experience aims to shed light on this reality and to guide readers toward a 'balanced mood for a balanced life'. I hope this booklet will be of help to maintaining a balanced life in the context of the many ways people may experience the ups and downs.

The Good Shepherd invites us to rest awhile among the grassy meadows and flowing streams. He wants us to relax in his presence – to be nourished, strengthened and renewed. In this place, we may turn from a closed fist of denial, frustration and turmoil to an open hand of acceptance, relaxation and serenity. After the rest, we may be invited to walk more closely with him, to be freer and more confident and to be better able to navigate the often-hazy path of our lives. It is true that we all need to work on maintaining balance in our lives, but we are not alone. We can learn so much from modern and contemplative wisdom to live life with great richness, and when all is said and done, we can rejoice that we are infinitely loved.

Ad majorem Dei gloriam
('To the greater glory of God')

CHAPTER 1

Upsides: Unexpected Blessings Along Our Mental Health Journey

RESILIENCE

How does a shoot spring from a stump? How does a person with a drug addiction heal from it? How do I get through my own disasters to reach a deep sense of peace? These accomplishments testify to the power of resilience.

In 2017, I was faced with the reality of another period of unemployment, and for those of us who have been unemployed, we know it's not an easy situation. However, I had a burning desire to write – I finished a first draft of a screenplay during my free time. It did not solve the financial problem of unemployment, but it helped to reduce the boredom.

Research reports that having caring and supportive

relationships within and outside the family help build resilience. Within my family, I surrounded myself with brilliant people during challenging times – I shared my faith journey with my mother, I met for tea with my sister and I sought mental health advice from my twin. Outside the family, I shared my burdens with close colleagues, I spoke with my spiritual guide about my relationship with God and I laughed with my friends. What's more, it was indeed a beautiful thing to believe that Jesus is with me always, until the end of time.

Meditation also improved my ability to adapt and be flexible to what life threw at me. Practising a stillness exercise in the morning led to peace and calm, encouraging me to stay strong in the face of adversity for the rest of my day. Today, I can use my gift of visualisation or imagination to boost my resilience. Saint Ignatius Loyola's *Spiritual Exercises* present a 'Contemplation for Achieving Love' which describes God's presence in creation: 'in every created reality, in the sky, in matter, plants and fruits, herds and the like' (SE, 236). When I try to find God in all things through this contemplation, I remember that God desires to dwell in my heart – to give me life in the Spirit.

I imagine using all of my talents in a fruitful career. I imagine married life and the great love and meaning that this brings. I recall the words of a childhood prayer of mine: 'Oh God, you bring joy to my heart'. The power and beauty of resilience lies not in trying to become completely free of our mental health struggles but rather gracefully learning to live with them. Perhaps then we shall see the shoot spring from the stump, with a pink flower, in full blossom.

=== ● ===

Reflect

Give a concrete example of how you responded to a challenging situation in your life.

Read

EPHESIANS 4:2–3

SUPPORT EACH OTHER IN LOVE

With all humility and gentleness, with patience, bearing with one another in love, making every effort to maintain the unity of the Spirit in the bond of peace.

=== ● ===

HUMILITY

I remember being alone in the dark. I came to an enormous tree, looked up and felt overcome by awe. I was suddenly put in my place and felt great respect for this force of nature, and that helped me to tap into humility.

My mental health can diminish from time to time, and this reminds me that it is not always in my hands. I can usually adapt, for example, to the seasonal changes, the high stress of festivities and feelings of loneliness. Sometimes, however, I have to submit to the unforeseen challenges that leave me unable to cope and be functional. Author C S Lewis said, 'True humility is not thinking less of yourself; it is thinking of yourself less'. As I sat in my chair waiting to see the doctor, I looked around to see many others who were suffering. Some may have lacked support of family, some may have felt lonely and some may have experienced physical health problems on top of their mental health challenges.

Humility, perhaps surprisingly, is a most precious gift: it relieves me of any perfectionistic pressures. It enables me to let go the reins of control and to listen more deeply to God's will for me. I can make decisions based on the reality of my situation rather than straining myself with what is not there. The Spirit moves me to write, so I write. On one occasion when I was at a low point, the cons of attending my college graduation outweighed the pros, so I declined the invitation. My instructor phoned me and said there was no pressure to make a speech but that he'd love to see me there. Something stirred within me. In the end, I made it to my graduation and spoke publicly for the sake of others. I applied the humility principle and surprised even myself.

It is also about having a true appreciation of myself. I ponder that I do not need to do anything for this to take place. I am right just the way I am. So, it's OK to feel powerless. It's OK to be vulnerable. What's more, humility is a central theme to the Christmas story. The infant Jesus is powerless yet held by the love of the universe. The participants who surround him think of themselves less: they gaze and praise. The three wise men follow the Star of Bethlehem until they greet the infant with gifts and bended knees.

≡ ● ≡

Reflect

What is it like for you when you are in a vulnerable state, e.g. low mood or overexcited? Are you able to humbly stay with this experience – on your own or in the company of others?

Read

LUKE 22:39–44

JESUS HANDS OVER HIS WILL TO HIS FATHER

'... *Father, if you are willing, remove this cup from me; yet, not my will but yours be done ...*

≡ ● ≡

WISDOM

I met Roshi Robert Kennedy, an old wise man, last year at the Dominican Retreat Centre in Tallaght, Dublin. He is one of the few Jesuit priests in the world who is also a Zen master in the Buddhist tradition. I met with him for career advice, but after talking he invited me to attend a retreat at the centre. Referring to the Zen retreat, he said: 'Come and sit, and see what happens'.

Over the weekend, I practised *zazen* (the act of straight-backed sitting and rhythmic breathing which help unify and control the mind through sustained concentration) with about thirty-five others. It can be difficult for people to quieten their minds and be still. This was the case for me as I found it challenging to maintain a reasonably comfortable sitting position and to stay with whatever thoughts, emotions and images came my way. We also walked in a meditative way and I processed the experience in between sessions. I felt a deep peace and gained a personal insight with regard to my mental health: that I do not want to use my condition as an excuse for not pursuing family life.

During my second Zen retreat, I tuned into the 'bursts of loveliness' which were seemingly hidden in the world. I rejoiced at dinner, for example, when my perceived cold mince pie turned out to be crumbly hot! I was grateful when my sudden drop of blood pressure during meditation re-awakened me with a boost. Even the potted Christmas cactus in the centre with wonderfully blooming pink flowers seemed to want to 'burst out in praise' in the midst of winter. I also began to appreciate more my own Catholic tradition as we celebrated Mass together. It was a marriage of Buddhism and Christianity.

Too many of us learn to 'love' distress and anxiety: we say it is the way of work and the world. Just five minutes of silence seems pointless. But we get in touch with the 'inner teacher' when we find times to be still in our day, connecting us with deep peace and balance. It is available to be tapped into as we live in the moment: talking to people, working on tasks, walking with a fresh breeze on our faces, even running. I am so grateful that I listened to the invitation of the wise man at the retreat centre. It has stirred me to stop fixing my eyes on the ground and see the beautiful ordinary.

Reflect

What qualities do you think a wise person embodies?
Perhaps someone you know comes to mind. How can
you get in touch with your 'inner teacher'?

Read

ECCLESIASTES 8:1

GROW IN THE LIGHT OF WISDOM

*Who is like the wise person? And who knows the
interpretation of a thing? Wisdom makes one's face shine, and
the hardness of one's countenance is changed.*

≡ ● ≡

≡ ● ≡

CHAPTER 2

Downsides: Challenges Along Our Mental Health Journey

THE INNER CRITIC

My mind can play havoc at times. As I look back on my day, for example, which was filled with ninety-five per cent goodness – good work, good smiles, good sun, good rain, good life – I suddenly sense a finger pointing at me. It accuses: 'You're useless. You are good for nothing. Why did you do this and that today? You should be ashamed of yourself'. Then I begin to crumble, and I feel tempted to turn to distractions that keep me from feeling good about myself. But another voice – at a deeper level – encourages me not to focus on condemnation but to let myself be showered with love.

The mindfulness movement, which focuses on living fully in the present moment, emphasises the importance of the 'inner observer'. From this perspective, I look at my life as if from the side of a river. The river can be like the world and my life like a boat flowing downstream. Instead of judging and criticising the events and circumstances of my day, I am gentler on myself. I take in the totality of my experience which includes seeing the ninety-five per cent of it that was good and the five per cent of it that was not, and putting each in their rightful places. If my inner critic attempts to interrupt my observing mind, I need to go back to the side of the river.

For me, one of the most beautiful verses in the Bible comes from Psalm 23: 'In grassy meadows he lets me lie, by tranquil streams he leads me to restore my spirit'. When I repeat it like a mantra, I am suddenly transported to another time and place. I am invited to rest a while among the meadows and streams in the company of the Good Shepherd, who is my everything. If I sense the finger pointing at me again, then I pause, smile and return to my mantra.

The more I nourish my 'inner observer', the more I am led toward peace and stillness. Acclaimed clinical psychologist Jordan B Peterson says that as we direct our lives more away from Hell and more toward Heaven – whatever that means for each of us – we replace shame and self-consciousness with the natural pride and forthright confidence of someone who has learned once again 'to walk with God in the Garden'. Surely that would give us a reason for getting out of bed in the morning. Surely that would be a reason for living.

Reflect

What helps you to get some distance from your thoughts when they are troubling you? What leads you to peace and stillness?

Read

PSALM 23

THE GOOD SHEPHERD LEADS US TO STILLNESS

In grassy meadows he lets me lie, by tranquil streams he leads me to restore my spirit.

— ● —

POOR SELF-IMAGE

We commit a fatal error when we compare ourselves to others, for example, in our career, relationships and life. When we do so, we fall into the trap of living through the eyes of others where we will never have enough or be happy. No one person is the same; we all have our own unique combinations of gifts and talents. A better way is to measure ourselves from who we were yesterday: in terms of love, forgiveness, humility, and so on. In the longer term, we can reflect on the fullness of our lives through paying attention to the expansiveness of our hearts and minds.

Sometimes the love that another person shows us enables us to further breakdown our poor self-image. They gently remind us that we are people of great worth and potential. They may sincerely compliment us, for instance, on our kindness and consideration, our preciousness, our positive effect on others. Their love nudges us to be more compassionate on ourselves and we start to shift to a more realistic perspective: we see our negative characteristics in light of our many positive ones. We shine a little bit more.

No doubt our faith in God stirs us to shake away any residue of self-destruction. In prayer, when we imagine God's kind eyes gazing at us, we may sense the divine light touch our hearts. We may become more grateful for the many blessings of our day. We accept the frustrations and imperfections and begin to smile with peace and serenity. We delight that God delights in us. We bask in our own beauty and in the beauty of others. We become companions of Jesus in a mission to build up the kingdom of God through fully expressing our gifts and talents.

When we see through the eyes of an enlightened heart, we come in touch with a renewed self-image. We have made the journey from learning to love ourselves to actually doing so. This has transformational effects on our being for we no longer operate out of fear and anxiety which imprison us. We find, for example, that we are more present and calmer with people and we feel the grace of God at work in all of creation. We increasingly desire to tune into the life and joy that God calls us to. Perhaps we make a commitment to positive self-image each day.

Reflect

How might you compare yourself to others? What
impact has the love of another person had on you?
What impact does God's love have on you?

Read

EPHESIANS 1:18–19

SEE THROUGH THE EYES OF
AN ENLIGHTENED HEART

*So that, with the eyes of your heart enlightened,
you may know what is the hope to which God has called
you, what are the riches of God's glorious inheritance among
the saints, and what is the immeasurable greatness of God's
power for us who believe, according to the
working of God's great power.*

━ ● ━

RELATIONSHIP DIFFICULTIES

We all run into relationship hurdles at some point in
our lives, perhaps on a continuous basis. At times, we
can be very sensitive to minor disturbances which can
lead to mental health problems. A disagreement, an
uncomfortable silence or a raw tension can tip us over the
edge toward insomnia, anxiety and vulnerable moods.
The reality is that these are normal interactions that we
must try to live with. To smile in the acknowledgement
that not everyone likes us may be an important first step
toward wellness.

Our appropriate use of touch is a key way to improve our relationship with others. We have a vital need for it, from our earliest moments to the end of our days. A handshake, 'high five' or friendly pat on the shoulder can draw us close to others. A hug, hand to hold or gentle kiss can draw us even closer. We would do well to reach out a little further the next time we are with someone, and to notice how we feel afterwards.

Moreover, taking chances on revealing ourselves is necessary for emotional intimacy. We need courage to share something personal, look the person in the eyes, build trust and go on a journey together. A silent presence can sometimes be enough – I recall an image of my grandparents walking in the park, holding hands without saying a word and smelling the roses. When we are thankful for our relationships, we are more ready to respond to deeper invitations of love.

Pope Francis spoke on the theme of relationships at Croke Park, Dublin in August 2018. He spoke clearly and simply about love and forgiveness in the family. He emphasised the need to say 'please, thank you, and sorry' to each other. He asked us to say the words out loud, 'PLEASE, THANK YOU, and SORRY', and to repeat them one more time. Everyone in the stadium spoke in unison, to which he replied in English, 'Thank you very much!'

He also pointed out how easy it is to be physically intimate with one another in appropriate ways. What are we afraid of? I used to hesitate to kiss my grandmother when I saw her every day. I clearly loved her through my words and other deeds, but I seemed to have saved my kisses for only special occasions. So, I followed the Pope's advice and started to do it, and it has now become second nature. Every day is a special day and an opportunity to show our love in the world.

≡ ● ≡

Reflect

Describe a recent experience when you felt close to someone. How does God see this experience?

Read

EPHESIANS 3:14–21

LOVE OF CHRIST LEADS
TO LOVE OF EACH OTHER

For this reason I bow my knees before the Father, from whom every family in heaven and on earth takes its name. I pray that, according to the riches of his glory, he may grant that you may be strengthened in your inner being with power through his Spirit, and that Christ may dwell in your hearts through faith ...

≡ ● ≡

=====•=====

CHAPTER 3

Recovery: Steps and Considerations for Getting Back on Track

SPIRITUAL GUIDANCE

An important development in my mental health journey came when I made contact online with a Jesuit spiritual guide a few years ago, after I had left the early stage of training for the Catholic priesthood. I bounced personal concerns off him from time to time. He always had a kind word to say and his gentle support prompted me to continue my mental health journey. Eventually, a lady from a young adult ministry helped organise for us to meet, and so began the process of spiritual guidance. I was a little nervous as I opened up to him, but I soon began to relax in his quiet, unassuming presence, and my confusing mood experiences were quickly understood and even cherished.

We met at mutually convenient spaces until we finally decided to meet at my guide's community house. I continued to open up, and at one point I disclosed a particular weakness that I had found prolonged my unstable moods. This was an important step in my recovery as he could then better guide me in his Ignatian tradition. He was able to suggest psycho-spiritual concepts that suited my situation and that led me toward a more fulfilling and meaningful way of living. Han F de Wit, author of *Contemplative Psychology*, notes that the strength of a contemplative tradition lies in its capacity for individual guidance, and I find Ignatian spirituality to be very strong in this regard.

For example, the Latin term a*gere contra* meaning to 'act against' or 'go against self' was a concept that perfectly applied to me. It is a form of training that helped me go against my natural inclinations, as I was often pulled in unhelpful directions. So, when I was in a 'high' state with a want for more buzz and excitement, I practised slowing down by going for a walk, turning off the internet and focusing on deep breathing. On the other hand, I pushed onward during a 'low' state when I felt like collapsing, by keeping to my appointments, spending time with my family and friends and continuing to pray. I also became more aware of the inner movements of consolation (being oriented toward God) and desolation (away from God), and in communion with the Church I came 'to know and to want what God wants'. Today, I see spiritual guidance as an essential part of the recovery process.

Reflect

Is there anyone in your life who helps to nourish your well-being and your faith in God? How can you ensure that you meet someone to give you the support that you need on a regular basis?

Read

PSALM 63:1

A DESIRE FOR SPIRITUAL GUIDANCE

O God, you are my God, I seek you, my soul thirsts for you; my flesh faints for you, as in a dry and weary land where there is no water.

—— ● ——

POPULAR TREATMENT

There are a number of steps a person can go through to recover from a mental health setback. Take, for instance, the case of someone who experiences depression. They may first contact a GP who listens to their symptoms and orders a blood test if deemed necessary. A referral to a psychiatrist may be recommended that usually involves the consideration of taking mental health medication. A lot of patience may be required to find suitable medication, which can differ from person to person, but they will hopefully experience a positive change in mood. At times, the person may need a stay in the hospital if they cannot cope by themselves, and this environment has the benefit of round-the-clock care and attention.

Further on in their treatment, the person may benefit from psycho-education with psychiatric nurses. They are taught, for example, to be mindful of their thoughts and feelings. Concentrating on their senses and letting distractions to pass by like clouds that come and go can reduce their stress levels. They may be taught to be more proactive in their recovery by identifying personal signs of distress, using wellness tools and contacting their support network. Regular psychotherapy sessions over a prolonged period may assist their personal development, for example, to be more assertive with people and to experience intimacy in their relationships. They may be inspired to become their own therapist and to take great responsibility for their wellness.

I recall some wisdom from retired psychiatrist Linda Gask who lives with severe depression. When asked about the most effective treatment for her condition, she said that it was not the tablets she has been taking for years, or her expertise and therapy. 'It's love,' she said, 'my husband John and the power of our relationship help me more than antidepressants or therapy. It helps that I matter a great deal to him, and he does to me. It's love, care, talking to him' (*Daily Mail*). We can take great consolation upon hearing her words, showing perhaps that the love of her husband mirrors the love of God. To contemplate God's love through the care of our support network surely enables us to dig deep and do the most loving and truthful thing in the midst of our mental health difficulties. Our only response, then, is to give thanks for our life and to live it well.

— ● —

Reflect

Are you curious about availing of treatment for you or your loved one? Perhaps you can browse the mental health resource section at the end of this booklet which provides information on related organisations.

Read

MATTHEW 7:7–8

ASK, SEARCH, KNOCK

Ask, and it will be given to you; search, and you will find; knock, and the door will be opened for you. For everyone who asks receives, and everyone who searches finds, and for everyone who knocks, the door will be opened.

— ● —

PAIN OR SUFFERING

The pain or suffering in our mental health journey can seem unbearable, to the point where we feel like God is not listening. My own struggle involved withdrawing in isolation from my colleagues and perceiving thoughts as if they were real voices. I believe through this vulnerable place that God wanted me to hand over my pain, accept help and be led into a different way of being.

I became a humbler person, in the sense of having a true appreciation of myself, as I made the necessary steps to recover. I was able to accept the bad days and to look beyond myself when I began to get stuck in the 'poor me' victim state. When I encounter pain, I now call out for the grace that wants to touch my heart. If I embrace the grace, I glorify God and become more fully alive. Sometimes I kick and scream out of anger and frustration, but ultimately I accept the reality of the situation. This points toward internal freedom, filling me with hope that I will see the sun on the horizon again. Grace also brings a clarity to my words and deeds.

I once meditated on the absence of Christ during Holy Saturday as part of my Lenten journey. I imagined that I was Nicodemus who helped cover the body of Jesus in linen cloths and spices. I prayed by his body and noticed a sense of loss and nothingness. I left the tomb, and, in my imagination, I prayed with my family. My Saviour's felt absence during that day reminded me of times of depression where God's presence seemed ever so distant. There was pain in those times, but the grace I received urged me to rejoice when my mood lifted like the rising sun, a reminder of God's glorious presence.

Saying what I have said about accepting my mental health condition does not for the slightest moment mean that I need to do it on my own. I believe that God is lovingly present and yearns to shower love on me. I have sensed God's concern for me over the years through the care of colleagues, mental health professionals and my spiritual guide. I have felt God's compassion through the care of my family and friends who have journeyed with me for better and for worse. These times remind me that God in fact deeply listens to me.

Reflect

What enabled you to accept, if even for a moment, the pain or suffering in your life? How does your faith speak to this experience?

Read

1 PETER 5:6–7

UNLOADING OUR BURDENS AND
ACCEPTING OUR PAIN OR SUFFERING
BRINGS CONSOLATION

Humble yourselves therefore under the mighty hand of God, so that God may exalt you in due time. Cast all your anxiety on God, because God cares for you.

CHAPTER 4

Balance: Modern and Contemplative Wisdom for Life

BALANCED LIFESTYLE

I recall something important from my time learning how to drive on the roads of Dublin. Whenever I came to a stop sign on the road, I put my foot on the brakes and repeated to myself: 'S … T … O … P'. Then I continued driving on my merry way. In the same vein, this is what I need to do when I come to the stop signs of my life. I need to respect myself enough to pause at junctures and to move forward with energy and vitality. I remember a particularly challenging period when requests for more work steadily increased. I was in demand for the first time in my life: to write this booklet on mental health for parishes and to write an article for the British Jesuits. I tried to make the most of presenting a series of reflections on Ireland's national radio and I kept to a rigorous six-day schedule.

Upon reflection, I realised that my desire to please everybody with regard to my career was a problem. I said an immediate 'yes' to extra work which clearly wasn't a good thing to do, as I began to burn the candle at both ends. Luckily, I spoke with my spiritual guide who kindly prompted me to get some awareness over my situation. I tried to fortify myself against any further plundering by STOPPING, and I stepped back from all the yesses. It turned out I could reschedule extra work, and I could be more vigilant of other requests in future.

Every day, I try to at least pop my head in to see my granny. Saying hello to her puts things into perspective. I could be the busiest and most 'productive' person in the world, but if I don't have time for my granny, then I am simply not living a balanced life. I was delighted to hear that she values me because I take the time to listen to her. It is people, not projects that count in this world. I am mindful of the words of Blessed John Sullivan (1861–1933) who encouraged us to take life in instalments and to do whatever we have the power to do. I commit to embracing that original lesson on the road and for the many opportunities to respect the stop signs of my life. So, please excuse me folks as I pop in to see my granny!

— ● —

Reflect

How do you know when you are becoming too busy?
Who helps you to maintain a balanced lifestyle?

Read

MATTHEW 6:25–34

LIVE IN THE PRESENT MOMENT

'… *So do not worry about tomorrow, for tomorrow will bring worries of its own. Today's trouble is enough for today.*'

══ ● ══

BALANCED MOOD

In his book, *Finding the Still Point*, Gerald O'Mahony presents a mood scale that is a bit different from our typical one. On a scale from zero to ten, he considers a score of five to be the optimal point of mood, known as the 'still point'. He says that numbers four, five and six are an experience of consolation, while the other numbers on the scale are an experience of desolation. Like the wisdom of *agere contra* in the reflection on spiritual guidance, if we're in a high mood, i.e., 7/10 or above, the best thing is to train ourselves to slow down – breathe, turn off the internet or the TV, connect with a friend who can steady us, turn to our inner strength. It is best to gently push onward when we are at the lower end of the scale, i.e., 3/10 or below. It takes guts, courage and heart to keep to appointments, go for a walk and remain warm to friends, neighbours and strangers.

We can look to Jesus in the Gospels as someone who exemplifies balance and stillness, for example, in the story about him and the woman caught in adultery (Jn 8:1–11). A noisy crowd of people bring the woman to Jesus, putting her in the middle so that all can see.

In their cunningness, they question Jesus about what to do with her declaring that in their law she is to be stoned to death. Jesus clearly loves the woman, as is his nature, but he doesn't fret about the situation. Instead, he starts to write on the ground with his finger. When the crowd confront him again, Jesus faces them and says: 'Let anyone among you who is without sin be the first to throw a stone at her'. They go away one by one, beginning with the elders, who are more experienced in matters of conscience. Jesus is left alone with the woman who is freed from being stoned to death. He calmly and lovingly tells her to go on her way. No fretting, and all is well.

Finally, finding regular times to pray is one of the best ways to enter into stillness. For example, in the practice of *centring prayer* we repeat our sacred word, e.g., 'Jesus', 'love', 'peace' slowly and steadily, enabling us to focus our mind and heart and anchoring us in the Spirit. We stop saying the word when our thoughts drop away, moving us to simply and profoundly rest in God. We repeat the word when our thoughts return, and so on in this manner. This contemplative experience has the capacity to transform our lives and nurture our being.

═ ● ═

Reflect

When you are in a vulnerable mood, how can you anchor yourself and return to balance?

Read

JESUS DOES NOT FRET, AND ALL IS WELL

'... Jesus bent down and wrote with his finger on the ground. When they kept on questioning him, he straightened up and said to them, "Let anyone among you who is without sin be the first to throw a stone at her". And once again he bent down and wrote on the ground ...

═══ ● ═══

BALANCED RELATIONSHIPS

My mother and godfather sent me the same video over the Christmas period. It featured the image of a train which served as a metaphor for a person's life. The person encounters many passengers, stations and conditions on their train journey. What struck me most was how sad it is when we fail to notice the people on the seats next to us. We may be too blind by our own preoccupations to simply lift our heads and see our neighbour.

Referring to God's will for each of us, Walter Ciszek wrote: 'The plain and simple truth is that his will is what he actually wills to send us each day, in the way of circumstances, places, people and problems. The trick is to learn to see that – not just in theory, or not just occasionally in a flash of insight granted by God's grace, but every day' (*He Leadeth Me*). How can we tune into what God wills to send us each day? How can we respond when the opportunity arises? I suspect this is somehow different for each of us.

According to Daniel Freeman, Professor of Clinical Psychology at Oxford University, there are five techniques to strengthen our relationships. It is thought that these can be used for building on the connections with the people we meet every day. They are:

(1) express our gratitude, e.g., when someone does something nice for us;

(2) make praise a habit, e.g., by complementing one person each day;

(3) remember what makes the person special, e.g., jotting down a few positive qualities and letting them know how we feel;

(4) be helpful, e.g., making a cup of tea or helping with a difficult task are great ways of building friendships;

(5) respond positively to good news, e.g., celebrating the person's achievement reinforces the bond between us (*You Can Be Happy*).

Finally, we can ponder that it is God who accompanies us on our 'train of life': whose Spirit wills to anchor us and give us joy. How can we refuse to greet our neighbour if we know this to be true? French mystic Gabrielle Bossis received an image of God as someone who watches for the direction in which the train will come from the platform at the station. 'That's the way My eyes are fixed on you,' she thought God said to her, 'waiting for you to come to Me'. What a beautiful image that speaks of a loving and compassionate God who is near and dear to us.

═══ • ═══

Reflect

How do you see God's will in the people you have met this week? How can you strengthen the connection with the people you will meet today?

Read

COLOSSIANS 3:12–15

WE ARE CALLED TO LIVE TOGETHER

As God's chosen ones, holy and beloved, clothe yourselves with compassion, kindness, humility, meekness, and patience ... And let the peace of Christ rule in your hearts, to which indeed you were called in the one body.'

═══ • ═══

CHAPTER 5

Loving Life: Fully Embracing Our Mental Health Journey

The reflections in this section are drawn from
the author's recordings on RTE Radio One's
A Living Word programme.

FRAGILITY

My late father comes to mind as I ponder fragility (from
frangere 'to break'). I imagine him looking at me and
wanting me to live a life of complete love. I admitted my
fragility at his grave. I called out: 'Dad, I have a problem
and I need your help'. He knows about the highs and
lows of my mental health experience. Surely, he has
encouraged me to act against elation and overactivity
– a common experience of the general public – and to
endure negative thinking and sadness. It was great to

visit his grave again because my sharing enabled me to carry him in my heart. He remains close and he knows the fragility of my family too: how apparent unity at one moment can turn into division at another.

As my friend and I bounced ideas about fragility off one another, she said, 'I think that often the gentlest of people have been through a lot of pain'. This hit me in the core as I have certainly become gentler through my pain. My struggles have seasoned me like the weather: eroding and smoothing my edges. When I was edgy, I was not very gentle. I reacted to the pain of the world with my own pain: I was sometimes challenging and willful. Now that I have endured the upsides and downsides of life, I am less afraid, more compassionate and loving. I want to gently reach for my friend's heart through my own brokenness.

Saint Hildegard of Bingen (1098–1179) used the concept of *Viriditas* or 'Greenness' to describe God's life-giving power. A power that courses through all of life, no matter how bleak the situation. She used organic images to illustrate her point including a tree that needs pruning. Just like the branches that are cut away in order to bear greater fruit, so too is the case for the shedding of my ego. As I let go of my own self-importance, be it with my career or talents, I expand my horizons and cooperate with the Spirit of the world. When I live my life according to this perspective, I am a more compassionate presence – willingly working with others, expressing my thoughts and feelings in respectful ways and ready to break out in laughter. I am thankful for my growth through pain because it has brought me closer to God and my human family.

≡ • ≡

Reflect

How do you listen to another person when they share their brokenness with you? How might you be gentler with them?

Read

JOHN 15:1–9

GOD INVITES US TO GROW AND BEAR FRUIT

'I am the true vine, and my Father is the vine-grower. He removes every branch in me that bears no fruit. Every branch that bears fruit he prunes to make it bear more fruit. You have already been cleansed by the word that I have spoken to you. Abide in me as I abide in you ...'

≡ • ≡

SELF-CARE

A story surfaces as I ponder the importance of taking care of our mental health. While on the bus, I got a tap on the shoulder from my neighbour Jimmy who wanted me to help a foreign woman find her hotel. She knew it was called the Hilton Dublin Airport, but she didn't know where to get off. From memory, I realised it wasn't actually at the airport; I told them it was in the Darndale area. Then, Jimmy and I had to get off at our own stop, so we looked around for anybody else who might have been able to point out the hotel to the woman. Another Dubliner was glad to help, and suddenly there were smiles and laughs all-round. We left the bus and the foreign woman happily waved goodbye.

As I reflected later that day, I realised that we went the extra mile by showing values of hospitality, community and fun. At the same time, I showed self-care by getting off at my own stop instead of staying on the bus and unnecessarily disrupting my day. Poor mental health partly surfaced for me as a result of giving too much and forgetting about myself. I broke down and I was brought to my knees in desperation. This time on the bus, I got the perfect balance between respect for myself and others, and I experienced a natural high. Each day, perhaps we can be mindful that self-care is key to sound mental health.

Pedro Arrupe, father general of the Jesuits from 1965 to 1983, originally introduced the motto 'men for others' (later it became 'men and women for others' and then 'men and women with and for others') for students in Jesuit schools throughout the world. While no doubt a very worthy statement – encouraging young people to develop a Christ-like presence – I think there needs to be a caveat attached. Saint Ignatius Loyola in his 'Rules for the Discernment of Spirits' warned people not to be tricked by the evil spirit, saying that it can manifest itself as an apparent good. For example, we may with good intention follow the motto with gusto – serving the poor, visiting the lonely, attending to the sick – but we are led astray by focusing so much on others to the extent that we reach burnout. Evil triumphs in such an outcome because by this stage we are no good to anyone. Pope Francis urges us to take care of ourselves by being faithful in prayer and staying in consolation.

≡ ● ≡

Reflect

How do you maintain your energy and direction throughout the day? How do you keep the flame of the Holy Spirit burning within you?

Read

ISAIAH 43:4
DWELLING ON GOD'S LOVE FOR US

Because you are precious in my sight, and honoured, and I love you.

≡ ● ≡

DISCIPLINE

Human energy is an amazing thing. Just recently, I wrote eleven pages of notes thinking about it: the energy we need for sports, for household chores, for performing the most complicated tasks at work, and so on. Our various spiritualities try to tune into these energies, to understand their dynamics and to channel them in the right ways. My mental health experience often requires me to redirect my energy. In line with established wisdom, if I become overexcited and overactive, then I need to slow down and focus on my breath.

At a family wedding in Galway, I tuned into the powerful force of gratitude: 'So my wish to you both', said a friend to the bride and groom 'is that when you wake each day, you will turn to each other with the same look you share today'. 'What a look of deep gratitude', I thought, 'for finding someone to share a life with'. I felt a wave of appreciation overcome me as the married couple came together to smile, kiss and dance.

In my experience, there is often a temptation to pull away from the ordinary emotions of living toward a world of passing moments and deep ingratitude. By prayerfully looking back over my day I can now appreciate a friend's smile, a meal from my mother, or a nice walk in the sun. It consoles me to ponder that we can channel our energy like saints in the direction of beauty, light and love.

Leonard Cohen (1934–2016) sang, 'There is a crack in everything, that's how the light gets in'. His words encourage us to expose our cracks – wounds, weaknesses, failures – so that the light of God can shine through and transform our lives. In prayer, we can present and offer up our many cracks. From one heart to another, we can express our vulnerabilities and raw pain, our sighs and disappointments, our true human selves. From experience, we know that God is very near to us when we are truly honest and sincere – it is the real Gavin, Vanessa, Samuel and Caroline that is needed. God showed the prophet Jeremiah that the faithful must let themselves be moulded again and again: 'Just like the clay in the potter's hand, so are you in my hand, O house of Israel'. We become instruments of light by being drawn into complete dependence on God and interdependence with others and the world.

≡ ● ≡

Reflect

How do you channel your energy like the saints in the direction of beauty, light and love? What is God saying to you through the setbacks and hurdles in your life?

Read

JEREMIAH 18: 1-6

GOD WANTS TO SHAPE US INTO A MASTERPIECE

The word that came to Jeremiah from the Lord: 'Come, go down to the potter's house, and there I will let you hear my words.' So I went down to the potter's house, and there he was working at his wheel. The vessel he was making of clay was spoiled in the potter's hand, and he reworked it into another vessel, as seemed good to him. Then the word of the Lord came to me: 'Can I not do with you, O house of Israel, just as this potter has done?' says the Lord. 'Just like the clay in the potter's hand, so are you in my hand, O house of Israel'.

≡ ● ≡

DEEPEST DESIRES

I used to think my deepest desires were as remote as the stars, and this perception contributed to depressive symptoms, i.e., a sense of darkness and gloom, which are common in the general public. Now, by looking at my concrete realities, I'm realising that what I really want is actually within my reach. I am learning that I need to place my feet firmly on the ground in order to wish, long, and yearn.

'The desires and longings which we have', said Bernard Lonergan, 'for what is beautiful, for what makes sense, for what is true, for what has value, and for what has ultimate value are at the heart of what it means to be human.'

In this effort to be more human, it helps me to think about a time in my life when I lacked true desire. In 2017, I completed a six-month internship in the civil service. In many ways, it was a very positive experience: working full weeks, attending meetings, reaching deadlines and using my gift of writing. However, when I thought about continuing this on as a career, I felt dry, unmotivated and a lack of joy.

So, I let myself be guided by my inner compass which has slowly pointed in the right direction. Now, I yearn to promote the psychological and spiritual needs of the general public, and one way I do this is through keeping a blog on mental health. I am close to the heat of my deepest desires without exploding and what a beautiful balanced thing that is.

Discernment, meaning 'to separate apart', is an important consideration for tuning into our deepest desires. There first exists discernment at the individual level which involves a level of spiritual freedom to make decisions. We can then look toward communal discernment or discernment in common which eventually requires a level of organisational conversion. We are always being called to go further, to open up into new life.

It is often tempting to make up our own mind on ordinary considerations in our family. If we want to be self-reliant, we may hang tight, be tough and carry on. While a certain resolve may be admirable, we do not become part of the bigger picture of building up the kingdom of God if we wilfully push through life with our blinkers on. Choosing to follow a common mission of goodness, beauty, truth, intelligibility and love surely satisfies our deepest desires.

═ ● ═

Reflect

What do you need to consider in making a good decision? Are you spiritually free enough to do it?

Read

PSALM 139

GOD UNDERSTANDS OUR DEEPEST DESIRES

O Lord, you have searched me and known me. You know when I sit down and when I rise up; you discern my thoughts from far away. You search out my path and my lying down, and are acquainted with all my ways. Even before a word is on my tongue, O Lord, you know it completely...

═ ● ═

I often wonder what makes a person stand out in a crowd. Two people may be brought up in similar environments, yet one turns to praise while another turns to sorrow. My Canadian cousin Conor, for instance, seems to have always had a sunny disposition to the extent that others are drawn to him, including me. While attending a college for people who needed specialist support, I was doing a project on what enabled people to be happy. It was advised, along with maintaining a healthy lifestyle, to spend time with happy people. I saw a photo of a young man with a broad smile and beaming eyes, and my cousin suddenly came to mind. 'I must spend time with Conor', I thought. So, I travelled to Canada on holidays and spent eight full days with him. I noticed upon my return to Ireland that I started to smile more and to experience glimpses of joy.

Saint Francis of Assisi, the great lover of the natural world, was almost blind and in a lot of pain when he 'burst out in praise' for all that had been given to him. 'All praise be Yours', he acclaimed. In gratitude, he created the song 'Canticle of Creatures' which refers to the sun, wind, air and fire as his brothers, and to the moon, stars, water, earth and death as his sisters. I further look to The Magnificat in the Gospel of Luke, where Mary proclaimed the ultimate 'yes' to be the mother of God. She inspires me to say 'yes' to God, just as I say 'yes' to my mental health condition. I call this personal prayer of mine 'The Magnificent Magnificat of Mary'.

Yes to your promptings, your movement within,
Yes to your inner light, your sunny sensualities.
Yes to her hands filled with openness,
Sing Hallelujah to her magnificent lowliness.

Yes to your gaze, your soft sensitivities,
Yes to your blissfulness, your heavenly mindfulness.
Yes to her eyes filled with pureness,
Sing Hallelujah to her magnificent blessedness.

Yes to your open road, your warm invitations,
Yes to your genuineness, your grounded worldliness.
Yes to her embrace filled with wholeness,
Sing Hallelujah to her magnificent fruitfulness.

Yes to your lion-heart, your brave inspirations,
Yes to your expansiveness, your meditative spaciousness.
Oh Yes, Forever Yes, My Goodness!

═ ● ═

Reflect

What is your favourite song right now? How would
you describe it... sad, ordinary, joyful?

Read

LUKE 1: 46-55

MARY PROCLAIMED THE ULTIMATE 'YES' TO GOD

*And Mary said, 'My soul magnifies the Lord, and my spirit
rejoices in God my Saviour, for he has looked with favour
on the lowliness of his servant. Surely, from now on all
generations will call me blessed; for the Mighty One has done
great things for me, and holy is his name...'*

═ ● ═

CHAPTER 6

Spirituality: An Inner Dynamism toward Fullness of Life

THE SOFT SOUND OF PRAISE

I was led into mystery last year through a study on the psycho-spiritual inspiration of three saints – Francis of Assisi, Hildegard of Bingen and Ignatius of Loyola. As an expression of my interest in spirituality and mental health, I investigated the mental-health-related factors that enabled the saints to 'burst out in praise' in the midst of pain or suffering. My findings included a psycho-spiritual development scale, factors of psycho-spiritual development and a representative model.

Early on, I thought that this 'bursting out in praise' process – also called psycho-spiritual inspiration – meant a real 'Hallelujah' moment where everybody would hear a joyful acclamation. While I do not deny that this can be the case, I began to understand the process as less obvious at first glance. Francis was known to have lived with two levels of experiences: one was at a surface level and another was at a deeper level. He experienced his own turmoil and anguish and the darkness of the world while at the same time he felt deep peace knowing that his pain or suffering was held secure by the goodness of the love of God.

Hildegard experienced the soft sound of praise in the midst of her mystical visions such as the vision of 'Soul and Body' which tells about the body and soul of the child coming together in the mother's womb. Her visions were supported by the pope of her time and by Saint Bernard of Clairvaux. Ignatius experienced this 'sweet softness' while contemplating on God at work in all of creation, as recorded in his *Spiritual Exercises*. His imagination enabled him to deepen his belief that God could be found in all things, everywhere in everyone, at all times.

The soft sound of praise can be compared to a heart that is strumming like a guitar or the deepest anchoring of Spirit. Like a lively contentment being around loved ones, doing ordinary things and experiencing ordinary emotions. I look to the image of a nun in the cloister who feels connected with an inner joy in the midst of solitude. She walks rhythmically and relishes the sunlight that touches her body. Her heart is big, and her spirit is deep. From this anchor of praise, we might just sense the energy of her smile, and perhaps after her quiet transcendence she will burst out like the sound of trumpet blast.

―― ● ――

Reflect

How might you connect with the 'bursts of loveliness'
right now? For example, the sight of flowers, a taste of
something delicious, a joy within yourself.

Read

PSALM 96:11-12

PRAISE GOD OF ALL THINGS

*Let the heavens be glad, and let the earth rejoice; let the sea
roar, and all that fills it; let the field exult, and everything in
it. Then shall all the trees of the forest sing for joy.*

―― ● ――

THE VALUE OF TIME

I had the privilege to interview a contemplative nun
for my studies, which revealed much wisdom from the
Christian tradition. Here, she talks about the value of
time and reached out to others, especially young people:
'Yes, the big thing is to give yourself time to be yourself,
give yourself time to enjoy things, give yourself time for
everything. You might have to make a conscious effort
to slow down but I think your life will change, life
nowadays is not healthy … In those days [Saint Francis
of Assisi], they had plenty of time.' I believe that these
words from someone who spends much of her life in
praise and in silence speaks of a core truth in our lives
today, and we may need training for this to happen.

She continues: 'Yes, when you're doing nothing you see your mind is processing all the things you have learned that day and you are getting them filed in your mind, where they should be. Whereas if you're learning the whole time, you haven't time.' Have you ever noticed that an answer might arise within your being when you put the phone down for a while – during a moment of doing 'nothing'? That is because your mind is doing what it's supposed to do without your conscious effort. It doesn't always need your help and googling to find the answer. Or you may find great peace and clarity after a long pause that enables you to live in the moment, and the next day you notice that your memory and concentration are better.

Saint Francis (1181–1226) lived in a time with more space and freedom to grow up. Although he had competing desires for what turned him toward God and for what turned him away from God, he did not have to face the challenges of social media, for instance, that can often decrease our face-to-face interactions with friends, family and strangers. He had more opportunities to notice the world around him. During a time before his conversion, he rode along on his horse and observed a man with leprosy on the side of the road. He felt repulsed by the man, but he got off his horse and forced himself to hug him. Today, our fears and anxieties may also surface when we pause for five minutes. Perhaps the next time we do this we can ask ourselves, 'What are our fears that we need to embrace?'

─ ● ─

Reflect

What happens when you find time to do 'nothing' in
your day? For example, *centring prayer*, looking out into
the garden, stopping when you hear the Angelus.

Read

ECCLESIASTES 3:1-8

THERE IS A TIME FOR EVERYTHING

*For everything there is a season, and a time for every
matter under heaven: a time to be born, and a time to die;
a time to plant, and a time to pluck up what is planted;
a time to kill, and a time to heal; a time to break down,
and a time to build up; a time to weep, and a time to laugh;
a time to mourn, and a time to dance…*

─ ● ─

The 'Bursting Out in Praise'* triangle shows that the development of three key factors – dependence on God, service of God and balanced mood – lead to 'bursting out in praise' in the midst of pain or suffering.

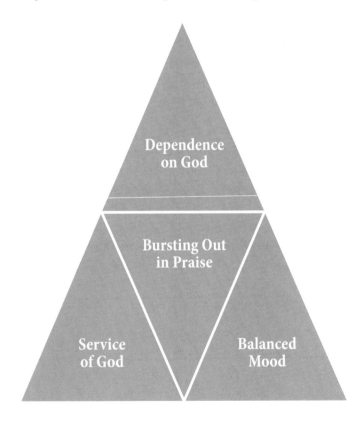

*'Bursting out in Praise' is short for 'Bursting out in Praise' in the midst of Pain or Suffering.

Dependence on God relates to a desire for prayer that expands a person's consciousness, an appreciation for nature in noticing the wonders of the world and the 'intuitive vision' where a person's pain or suffering is held secure.

Service of God relates to a desire for service of others beginning with minor steps; a lifestyle of praise that can seep into the soul and selflessness through a habit of self-emptying and service.

Balanced mood relates to a desire to let go (wherein the person hands over their pain and accepts help), the life-giving power of hope no matter how bleak the situation and loving-compassion in experiencing the emotional states of others.

It is thought that the Spirit guides us toward these key factors so that we may transcend our pain or suffering.

A person may develop to such a degree that their mind and heart expands, thus becoming fully aware of themselves and others. They see the world with fresh eyes, secure and rooted in concrete reality. They fully accept and embrace their world; they are in tune with the potentiality of all things, and they are completely active in building up their community. They are the embodiment of Ignatius's definition of love, 'Love consists in sharing what one has and what one is with those one loves. Love ought to show itself in deeds more than in words'.

It is delightful to ponder that the same Spirit that gives life in the mother's womb today existed in the womb of Mary. The Spirit, nurtured through good parenting and a regular prayer life, desires to guide the child through the inevitable challenges that come their way. The Spirit also wants them to grow in love, be of service and experience deep peace. Pedro Arrupe prayed to see everything with 'new eyes' and for a 'clarity of understanding' in the world. His fresh perspective was not a sort of 'pie in the sky' theology, but one based on concrete experience that spurred him to establish, for example, the Jesuit Refugee Service. Perhaps he was also able to 'burst out in praise' in the midst of pain or suffering.

═ ● ═

Reflect

How can you nurture the Spirit within you?
How might the Spirit want to lead you to 'burst out in praise' in the midst of your pain or suffering?

Read

PSALM 145
TO 'BURST OUT IN PRAISE'

I will extol you, my God, and bless your name for ever and ever. Every day I will bless you, and praise your name for ever and ever. Great is God, and greatly to be praised; God's greatness is unsearchable...

═ ● ═

All Ireland Spiritual Guidance Association (AISGA)

AISGA assists people in finding a spiritual guide. A spiritual guide accompanies a person on their spiritual journey, befriends their spirit and enters into the spiritual process with the person in ways that foster spiritual growth in all of the realities of their life. See www.aisga.ie for contact numbers and for more information.

Aware

Aware provides support and information for people who experience depression or bipolar disorder and their concerned loved ones. Freephone 1800 80 48 48. See www.aware.ie for more information.

GROW

GROW helps people who have suffered, or are suffering, from mental health problems. They provide a space to explore a person's relationship with God or higher power. Phone 1890 474 474. See www.grow.ie for more information.

Health Service Executive (HSE)

The HSE provides all of Ireland's public health services in hospitals and communities across the country. In consultation with the person's GP, they may be referred to their local mental health service including possible access to a psychiatrist, psychiatric nurse and psychologist. Phone 1850 24 1850 or 041 685 0300. See www.hse.ie for more information.

Irish Association for Counselling & Psychotherapy (IACP)

Counselling & Psychotherapy. Phone 01 230 3536. See www.iacp.ie for more information.

Irish Council for Psychotherapy (ICP)

Counselling & Psychotherapy. Phone 01 905 8698. See www.psychotherapycouncil.ie for more information.

Jigsaw (Young people's health in mind)

Jigsaw is the national centre for youth mental health. They are there to ensure that no young person feels alone, isolated and disconnected from others around them. They provide vital supports to young people with their mental health by working closely with communities across Ireland. See www.jigsaw.ie for contact numbers and for more information.

MyMind Centre for Mental Wellbeing

MyMind Centre for Mental Wellbeing provides counselling and psychotherapy face to face in Dublin, Limerick and Cork, and online. Phone 076 680 1060. See www.mymind.org for more information.

Pieta House

Pieta House is a non-profit organisation providing a specialised treatment programme for people who have suicidal ideation or who participate in self harming behaviours. Freephone 1800 247 247. See www.pieta.ie for more information.

Samaritans

Samaritans offer emotional support 24/7, 365 days a year on freephone 116 123 and by email jo@samaritans.ie. See www.samaritans.ie for more information.

Shine

Shine aims to empower people with mental ill health and their families through support, information and education while also advocating for social change. See www.shine.ie for contact numbers and for more information.

Turn2Me

Turn2Me is an online service that provides a 3 tiered approach to supporting mental well-being – self help, support groups and professional support. See www.turn2me.org.